100
PAPER PIECED
QUILT BLOCKS

by Linda Causee

If you love foundation piecing, but don't enjoy copying each block over and over so that you have enough patterns to complete the project requirements, you'll enjoy this book and its accompanying CD. Just pop the CD into your computer, click on the desired block in the size you want and print out all of the paper patterns you'll need for an entire bed-sized quilt, a wall hanging or even a miniature quilt. If you've never tried foundation piecing where every piece meets every other piece perfectly and where even the smallest block can be made quickly and easily, now is the time to try it with this new, easy method of procuring the required blocks.

LEISURE ARTS, INC
Little Rock, Arkansas

Produced by

Production Team

Creative Directors: Jean Leinhauser and
Rita Weiss

Photography: Carol Wilson Mansfield

Book Design: Linda Causee

Copy Editor: Ann Harnden

Pattern Testers: Hope Adams, Shirley
Cushing, Linda Ferguson,
Wanda MacLachlan, and
Christina Wilson

Machine Quilting: Faith Horsky

Contents

Before You Start

Choose the block that you want to make. In the front of this book, you will find a CD that contains the 100 paper pieced quilt blocks in 7 different sizes. Before you begin your project, follow the simple instructions contained in the CD.

When you are ready to make your quilt, simply print out the required number of blocks and start. No more tedious tracing or copying blocks!

The blocks on the CD are given as 2", 3", 4", 5", 6", 7", and 8". If you would like your blocks to be larger, use the following guidelines:

9" - use 3" block, enlarge 300%
10" - use 5" block, enlarge 200%
11" - use 3" block, enlarge 367%
12" - use 6" block, enlarge 200%
13" - use 4" block, enlarge 325%
14" - use 7" block, enlarge 200%
15" - use 5" block, enlarge 300%
16" - use 6" block, enlarge 200%

Traditional Blocks

Chicago Geese Bed Quilt

Chicago Geese Bed Quilt

Size: 85" x 95"   Block: Chicago Geese (page 8)
Number of Blocks: 56   Block Size: 10" finished

MATERIALS

$3/4$ yard each, purple, blue, black/orange print
$1/4$ yard each, orange, black/green print
$5/8$ yard each, red, green
1 yard black/purple print (includes second border)
$2^1/2$ yards black/blue print (includes fourth border)
$2^1/4$ yards black/red print (includes third border)
$1^1/2$ yards black/gold print
1 yard gold (includes first border)
$6^1/2$ yards backing
$3/4$ yard binding

CUTTING

8 strips, 2"-wide, gold (first border)
*9 strips, $2^1/2$"-wide, black/purple print (second border)
*9 strips, $1^1/2$"-wide, black/red print (third border)
*9 strip, $3^1/2$"-wide, black/blue print (fourth border)
9 strips, $2^1/2$"-wide, binding

*Sew the second, third and fourth border strips together and attach to quilt top as a single border.

Chicago Geese Wall Hanging

Size: 33" x 33"   Block: Chicago Geese (page 8)
Number of Blocks: 16   Block Size: 6" finished

MATERIALS

$1/4$ yard each, light red, light yellow, dark yellow, dark blue
$1/8$ yard each, dark red, dark orange, dark green
$3/8$ yard light orange
$3/4$ yard light purple (includes first border)
$1/2$ yard dark purple (includes second border)
$5/8$ yard light blue (includes third border)
$1/2$ yard light green (includes binding)
1 yard backing

CUTTING

2 strips, 2" x $24^1/2$", light purple (first border)
2 strips, 2" x $27^1/2$", light purple (first border)
2 strips, 1" x $27^1/2$", dark purple (second border)
2 strips, 1" x $28^1/2$", dark purple (second border)
2 strips, 2" x $28^1/2$", light blue (third border)
2 strips, 2" x $33^1/2$", light blue (third border)
4 strips, $2^1/2$"-wide, light green (binding)

Chicago Geese Miniature

Size: $11^1/2$" x $11^1/2$"   Block: Chicago Geese (page 8)
Number of Blocks: 16   Block Size: 2" finished

MATERIALS

Fat quarters of 6 shades of blue/silver prints (white to dark blue)
$1/8$ yard white/silver (first border)
$1/4$ yard dark blue/silver (includes second border, binding)
13" square backing

CUTTING

2 strips, $1^1/4$" x $8^1/2$", white/silver (first border)
2 strips, $1^1/4$" x 10", white/silver (first border)
2 strips, $1^1/2$" x 10", dark blue/silver (second border)
2 strips, $1^1/2$" x $12^1/2$", dark blue/silver (second border)
2 strips, $2^1/2$"-wide, dark blue/silver (binding)

Chicago Geese Wall Hanging

Chicago Geese Miniature   5

Log Cabin

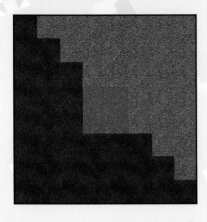

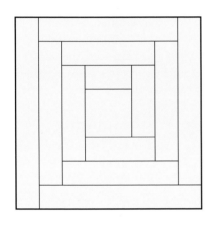

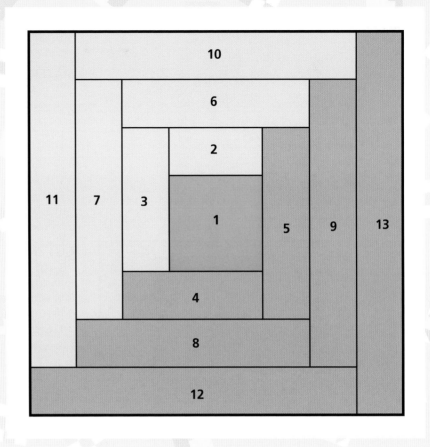

Pineapple

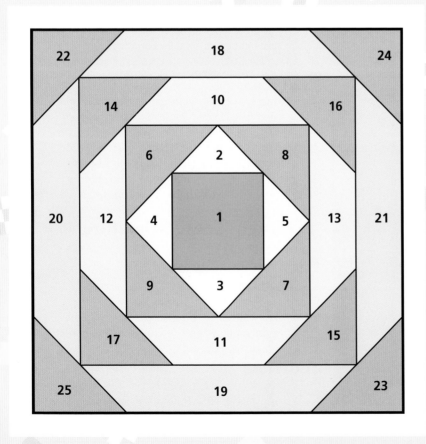

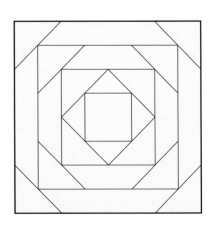

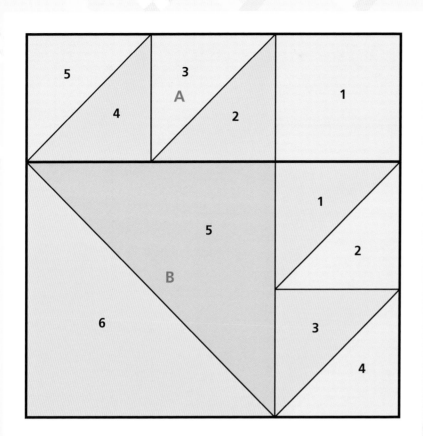

Cake Stand

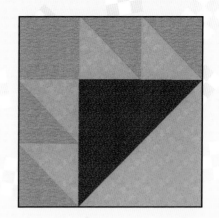

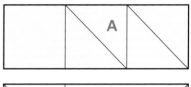

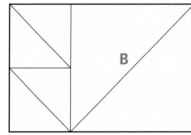

Attic Window

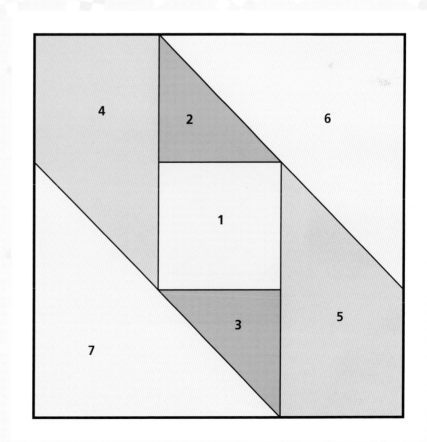

7

Chicago Geese

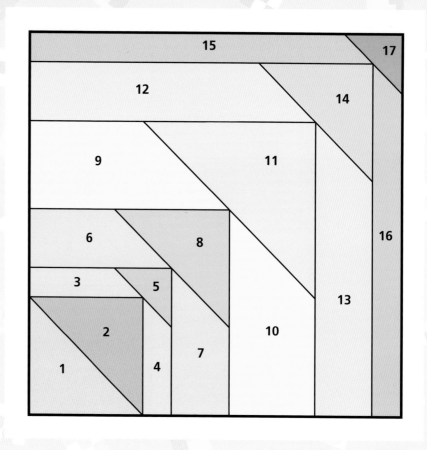

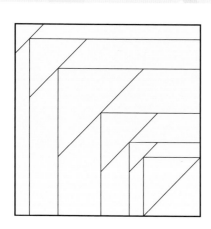

Snail's Trail

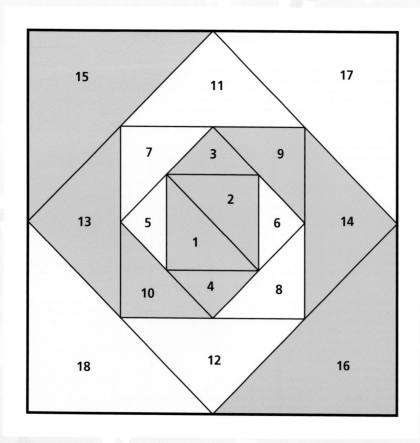

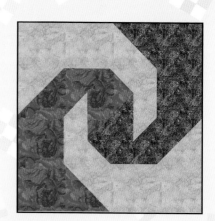

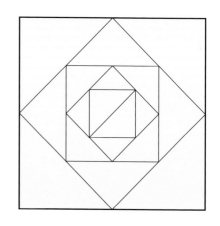

Cabin Flower

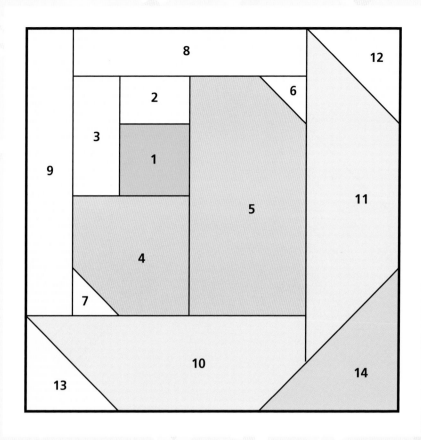

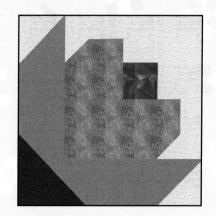

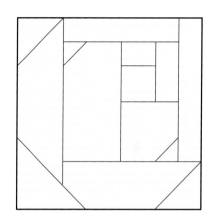

Bow Tie

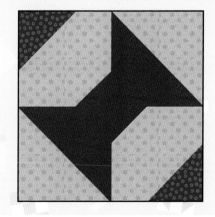

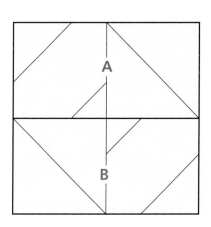

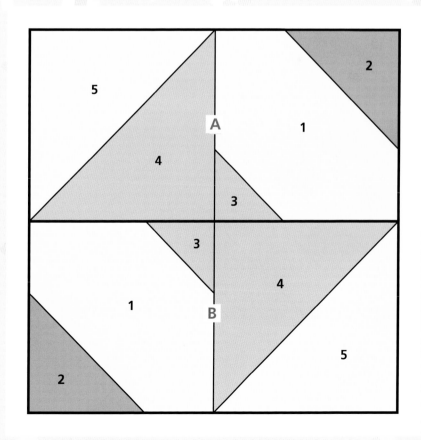

Zigzag

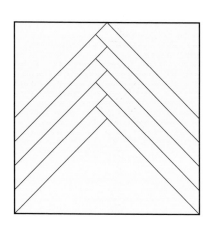

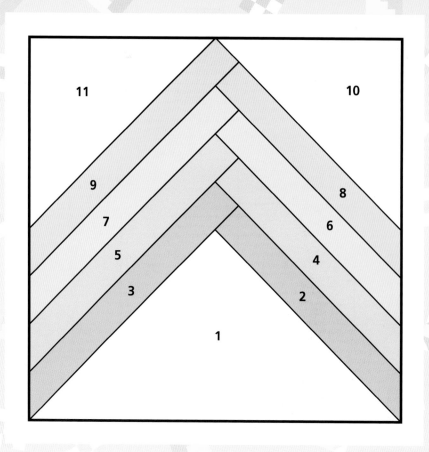

11

10

9

8

7

6

5

4

3

2

1

Chevron Ripple

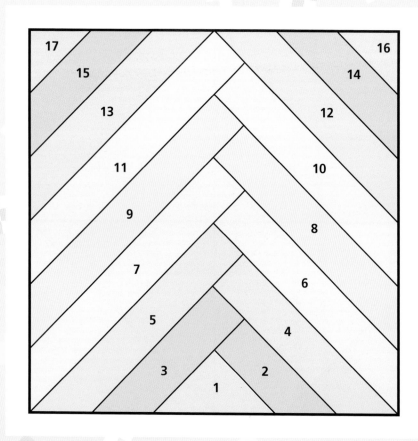

17

15

13

11

9

7

5

3

1

16

14

12

10

8

6

4

2

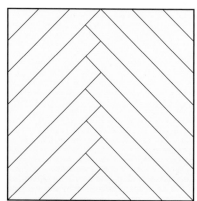

Tulips

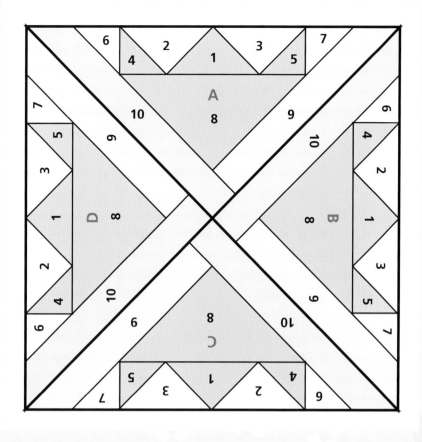

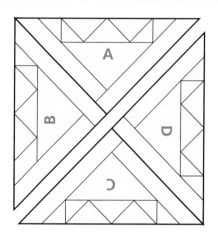

Flying Geese

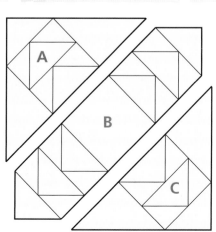

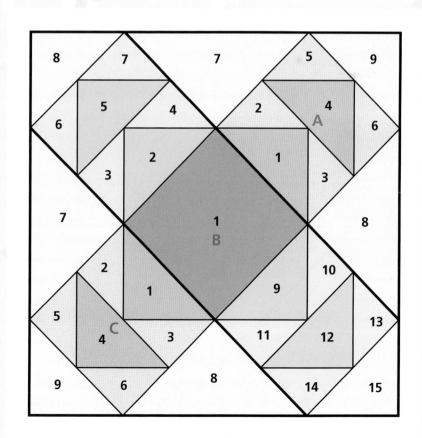

11

Four Patch

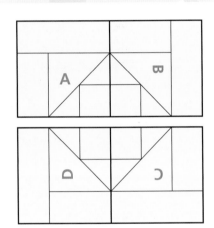

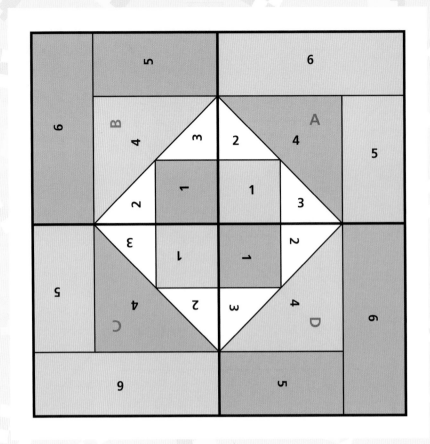

Basket Weave

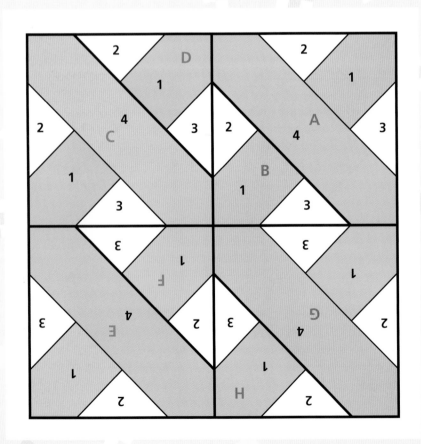

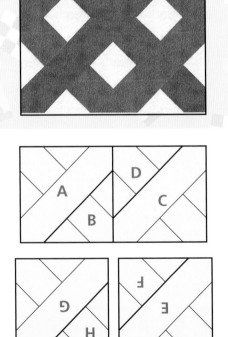

12

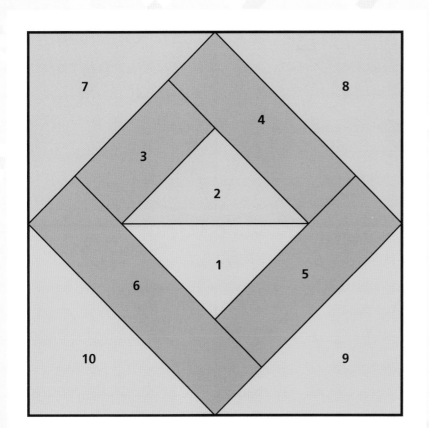

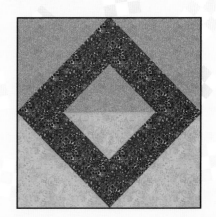

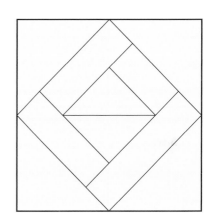

Pieced Triangles

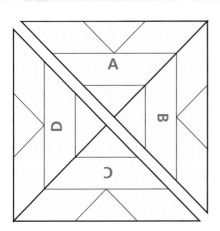

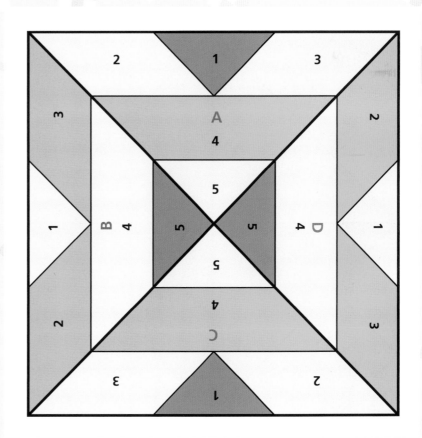

13

Starflower

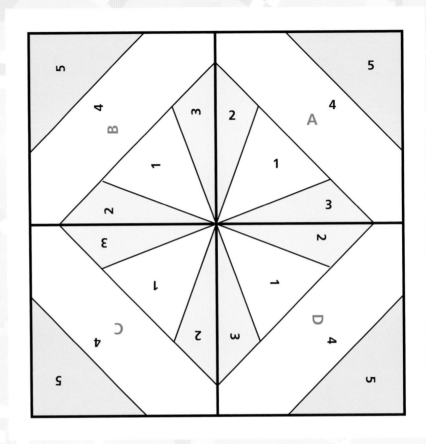

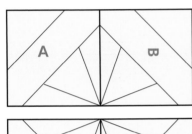

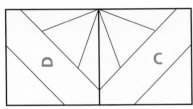

Ladies Aid

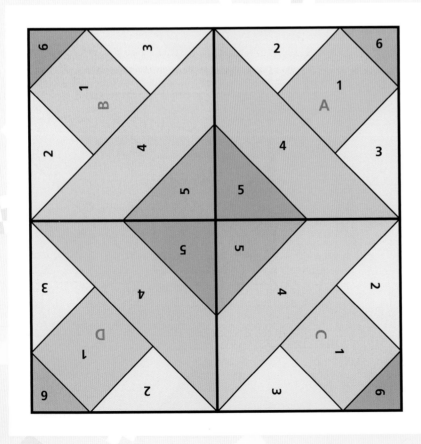

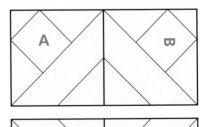

14

Follow the Leader

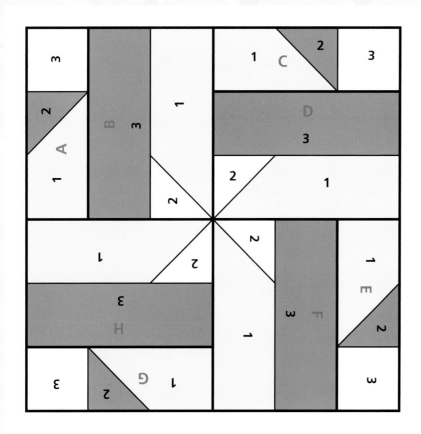

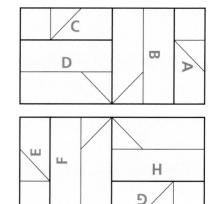

Wandering Geese

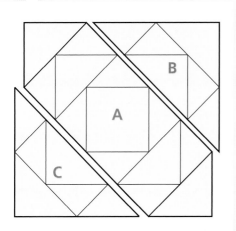

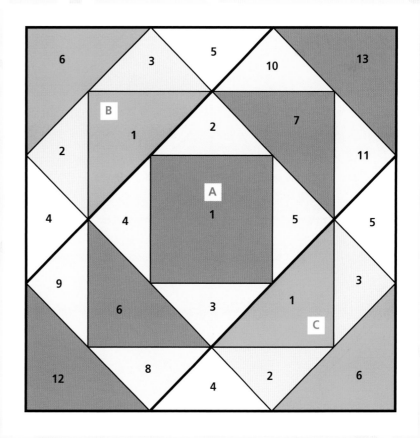

Hidden Flower

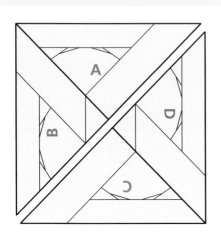

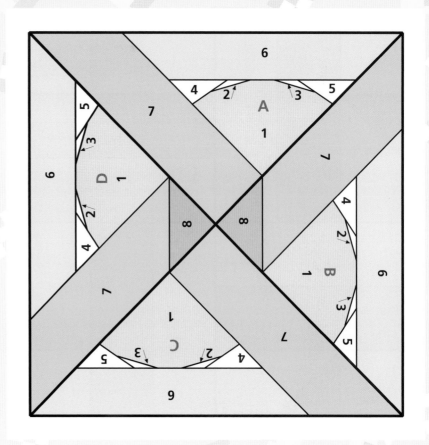

Robbing Peter

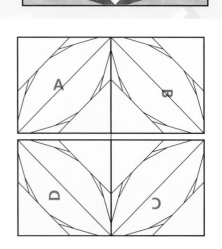

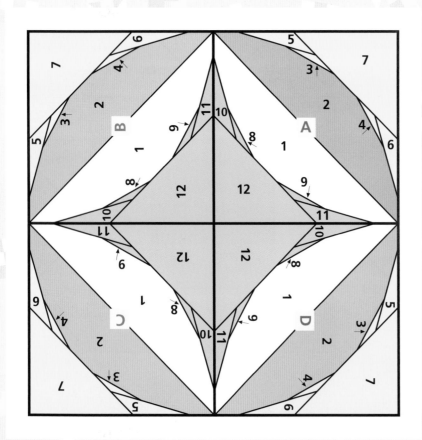

Travel Blocks

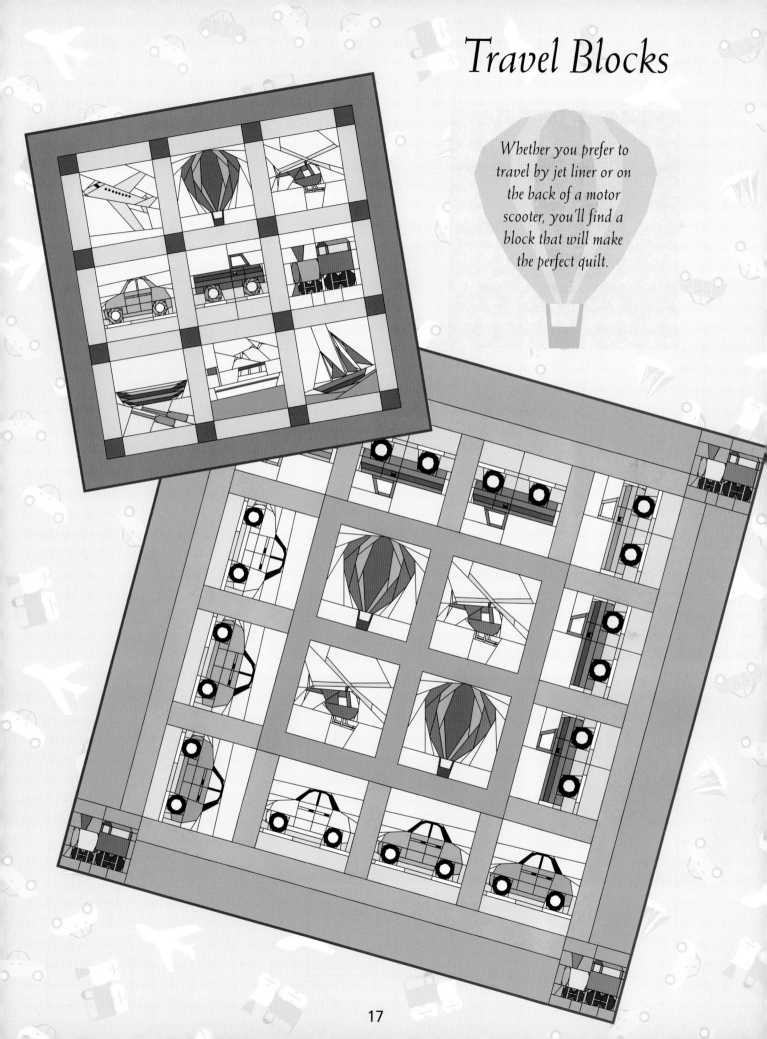

Whether you prefer to travel by jet liner or on the back of a motor scooter, you'll find a block that will make the perfect quilt.

Canoe

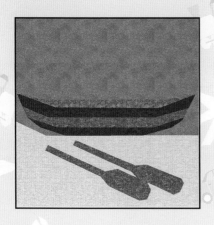

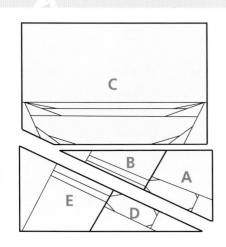

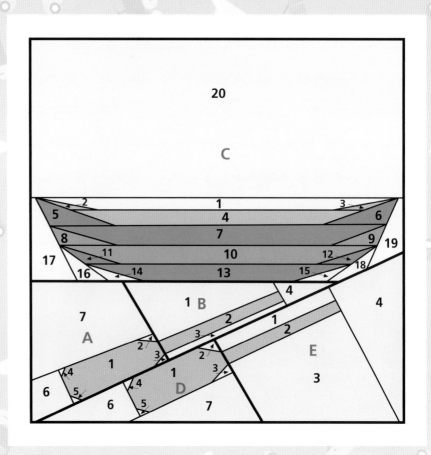

Helicopter

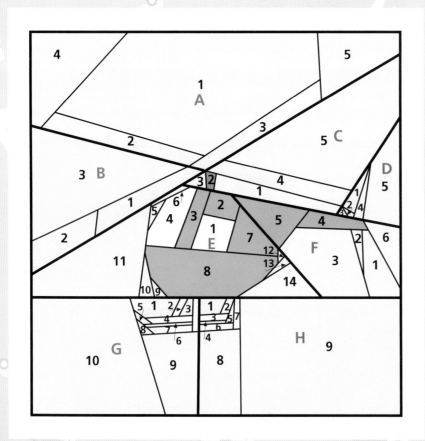

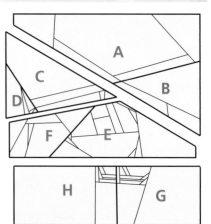

Yacht

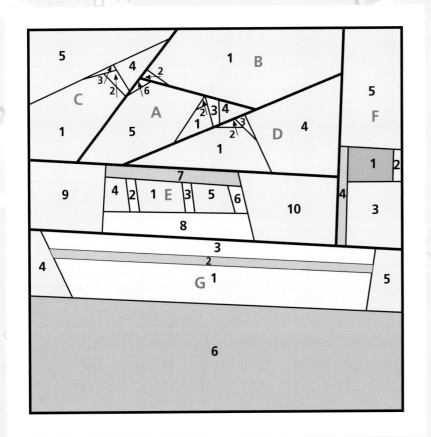

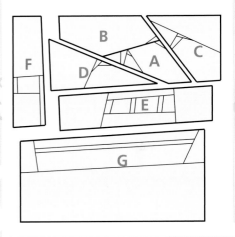

Motor Scooter

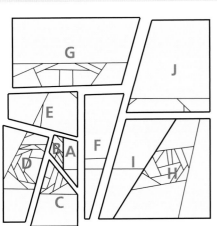

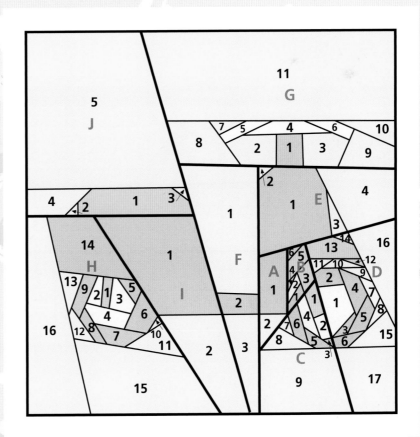

Train

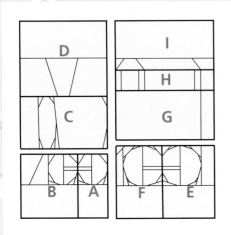

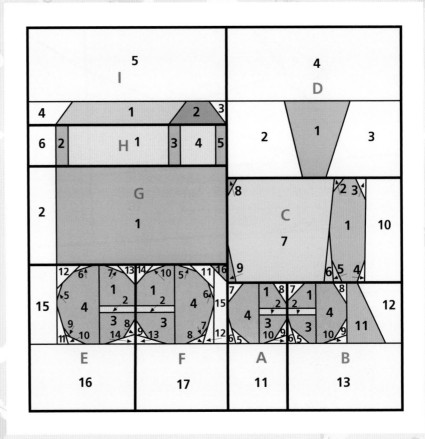

Car

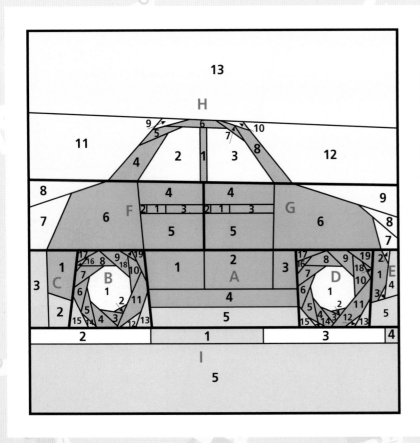

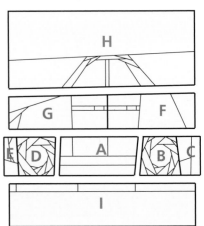

20

Jetliner

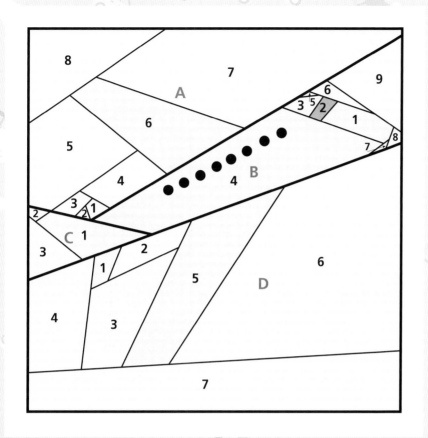

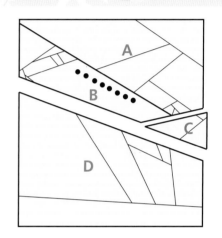

Pick-up Truck

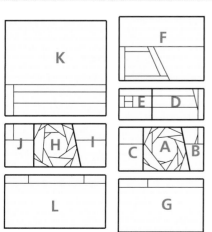

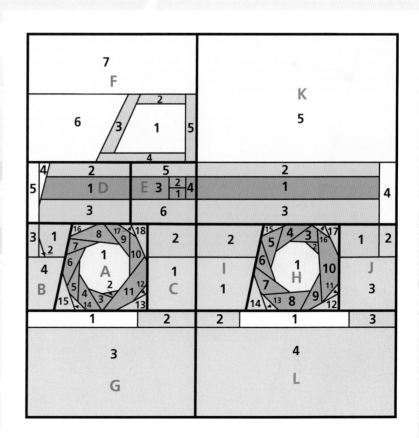

Bicycle

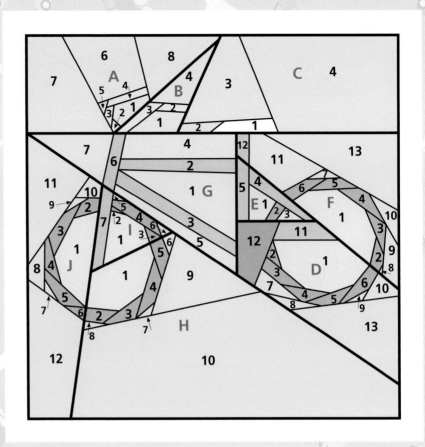

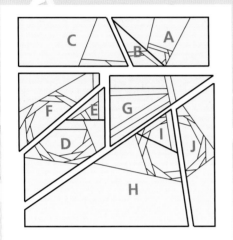

Scooter

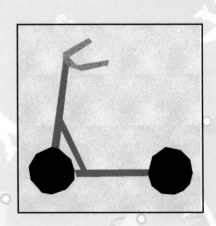

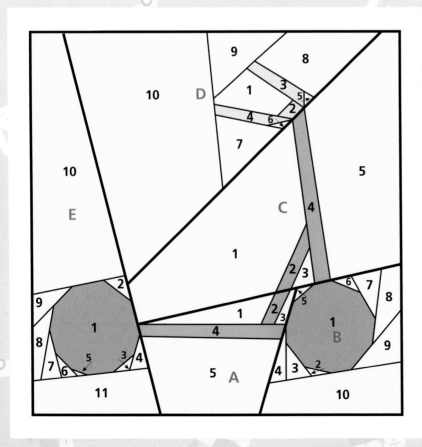

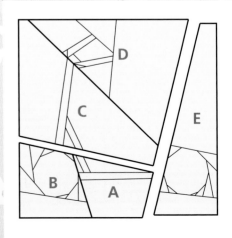

Hot Air Balloon

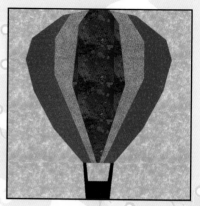

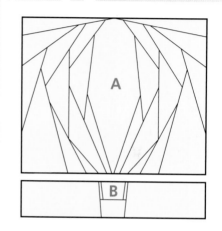

Sailboat

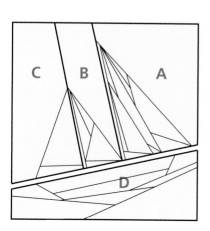

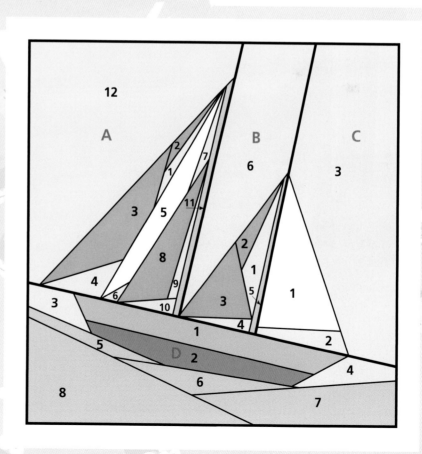

Curved Blocks

Medallion 2 Bed Quilt

Shied away from making curved blocks because you thought they were too difficult?

Not when you can use these blocks!.

Medallion 2 Bed Quilt

Size: 72" x 82" Block: Medallion 2 (page 29)
Number of Blocks: 42 Block Size: 10" finished

MATERIALS
1½ yards white
1½ yards light aqua
2½ yards medium aqua (includes first border)
4 yards dark aqua (includes second border and binding)
1½ yards medium blue
1¼ yards light blue
5 yards backing

CUTTING
8 strips, 2½"-wide, medium aqua (first border)
8 strips, 4½"-wide, dark aqua (second border)
8 strips, 2½"-wide, dark aqua (binding)

Medallion 2 Wall Hanging

Size: 39½" x 39½" Block: Medallion 2 (page 29)
Number of Blocks: 36 Block Size: 5" finished

MATERIALS
1 yard dark red
1¾ yards dark blue (includes second border and binding)
1½ yards white (includes first border)
1 yard light blue
1¼ yards backing

CUTTING
2 strips, 2" x 30½", white (first border)
2 strips, 2" x 33½", white (first border)
2 strips, 3½" x 33½", dark blue (second border)
2 strips, 3½" x 39½", dark blue (second border)
4 strips, 2½"-wide, dark blue (binding)

Medallion 2 Miniature

Size: 11" x 11" Block: Medallion 2 (page 29)
Number of Blocks: 16 Block Size: 2" finished

MATERIALS
Fat quarters of light yellow, dark yellow, light blue, medium blue
Fat quarter orange (includes first border)
½ yard purple (includes second border, binding and backing)

CUTTING
2 strips, 1" x 8½", orange (first border)
2 strips, 1" x 9½", orange (first border)
2 strips, 1½" x 9½", purple (second border)
2 strips, 1½" x 11½", purple (second border)
2 strips, 2½"-wide, purple (binding)

Medallion 2 Wall Hanging

Medallion 2 Miniature

25

Curved Pinwheel

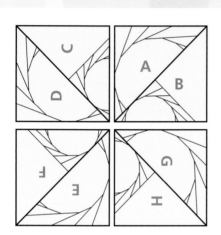

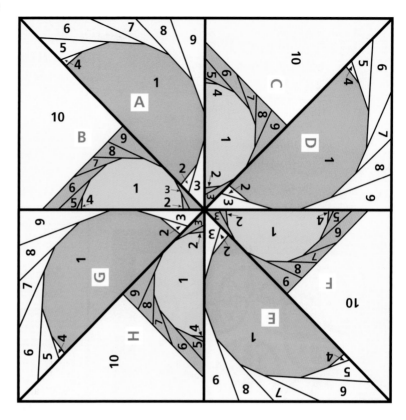

Posy

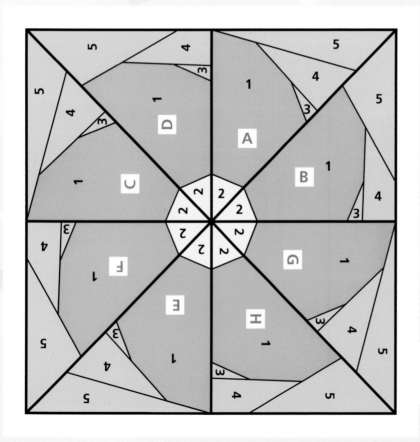

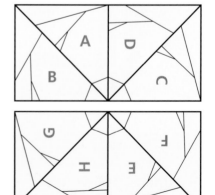

Curved Cabin

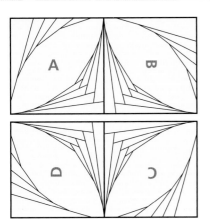

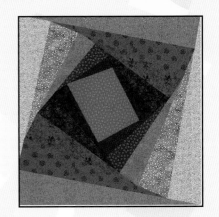

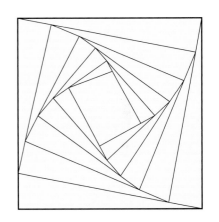

Curved Star

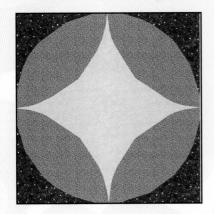

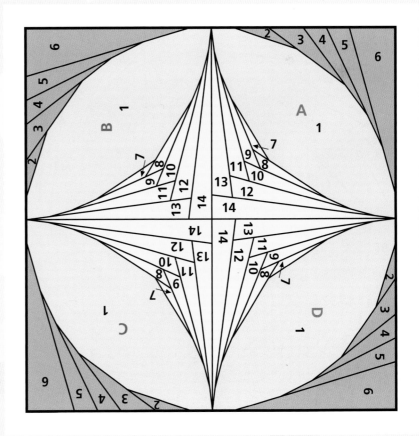

Medallion 1

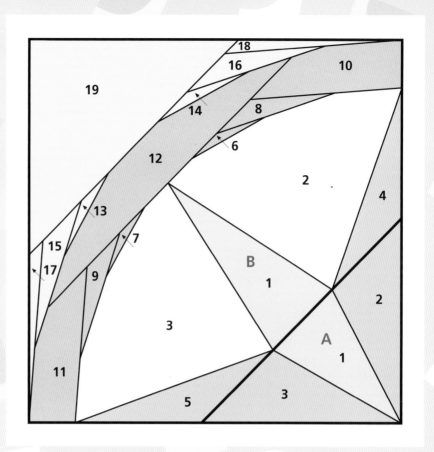

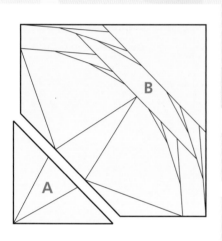

Patriotic Pinwheel

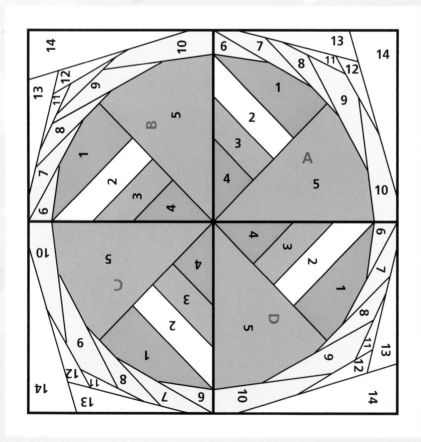

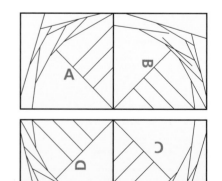

Fan

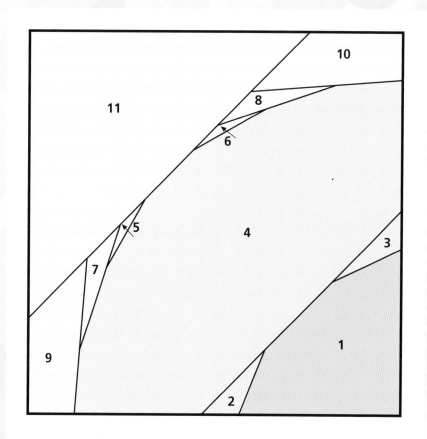

11
10
8
6
5
7
9
4
3
1
2

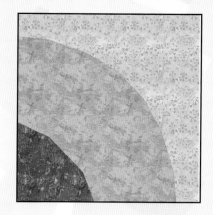

Medallion 2

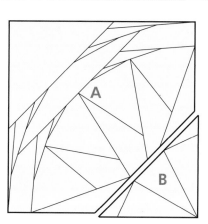

A
B

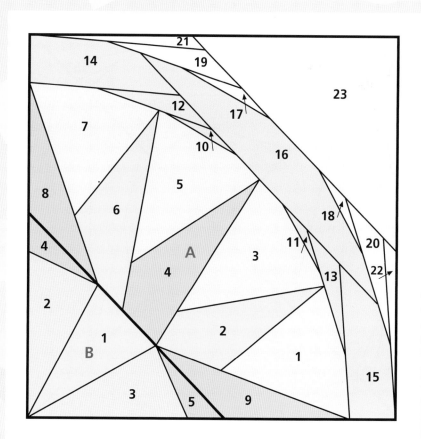

21
14
19
12
23
7
17
10
8
16
5
6
A
4
3
18
20
4
11
22
2
13
B 1
2
1
3 5 9 15

29

Pickle Dish

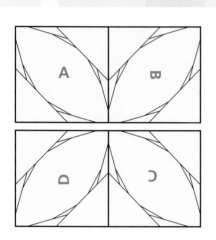

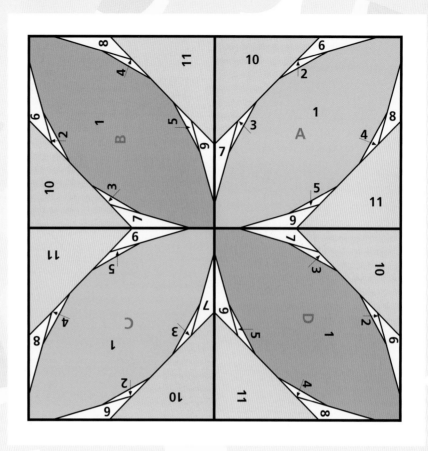

Circles & Squares

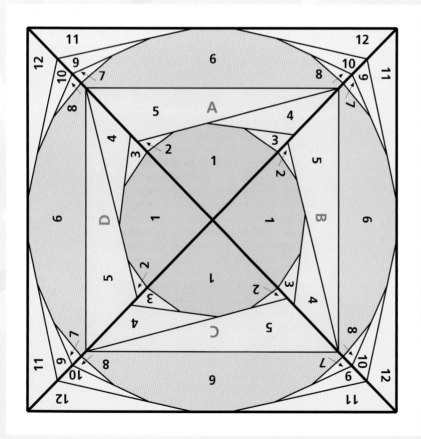

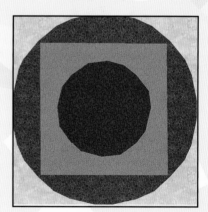

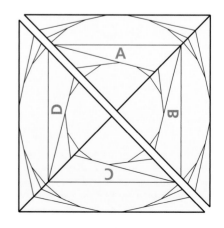

Calendar Blocks

Pick the block that celebrates an important day: a birthday, an anniversary, or just the month you started making quilts, and make a fun quilt.

Snowflake

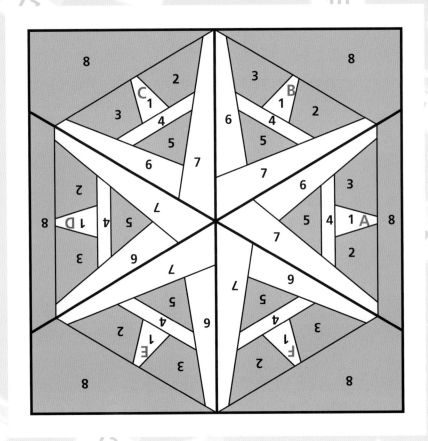

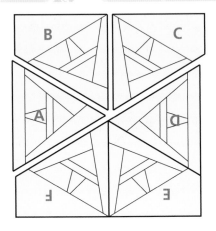

February

Hearts

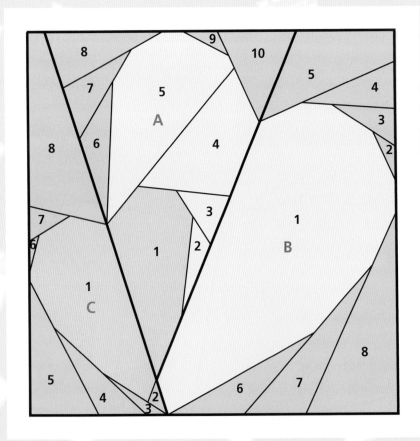

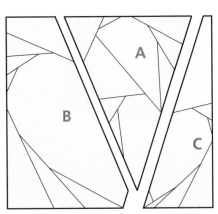

Leprechaun Hat

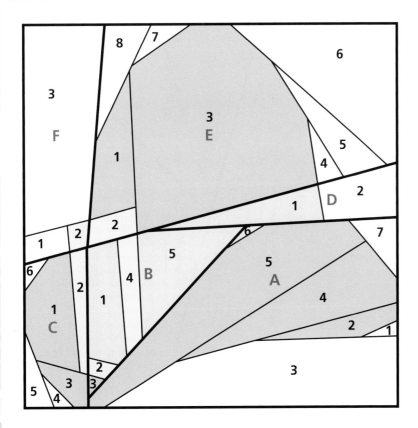

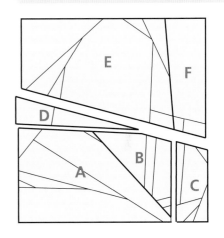

Easter Egg

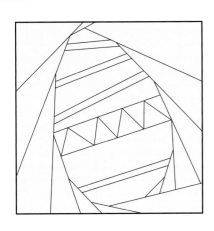

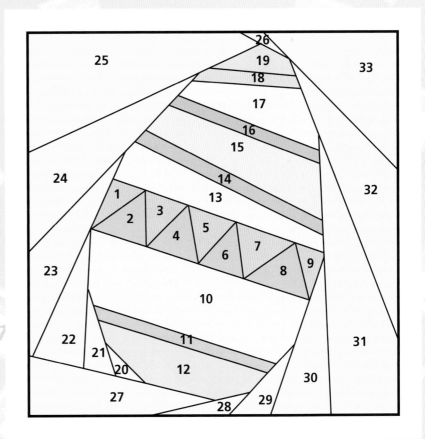

May
Mom's Flower

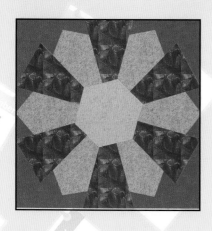

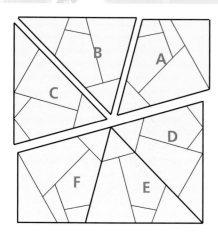

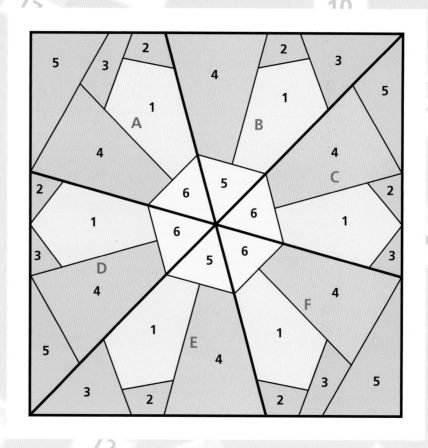

June
Shirt & Tie for Dad

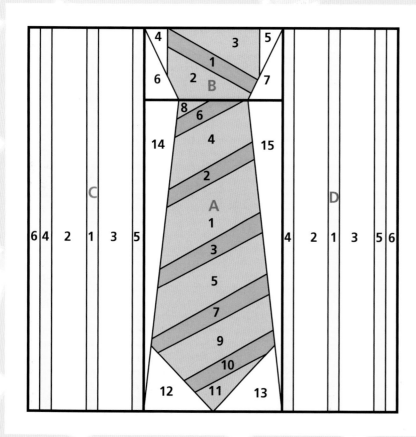

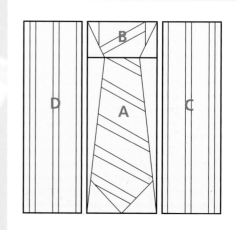

July
Skyrocket

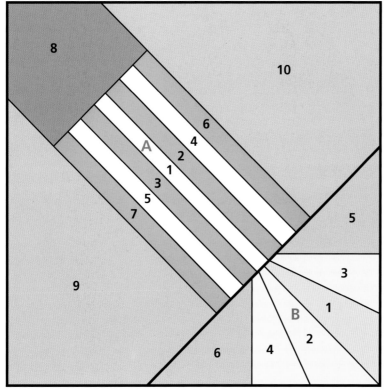

8

10

6

4

A

2

1

3

5

7

9

5

3

B

1

6

4

2

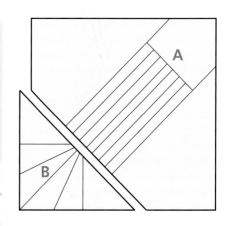

A

B

August
Beach Sandals

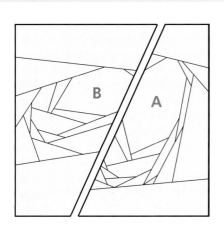

B

A

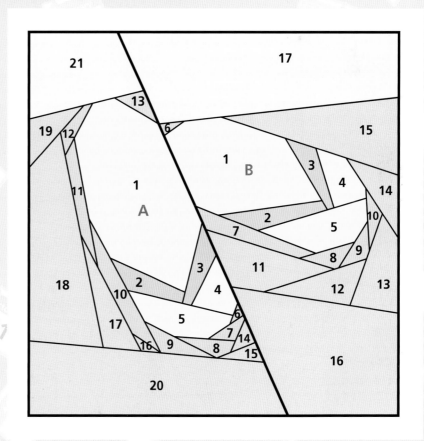

21

17

13

19 12

6

15

11

1
B

3

4

1
A

2

5

14

7

10

8 9

11

18

3

12 13

2

4

10

5

6

17

7

16 9

14

8

15

16

20

35

School Days

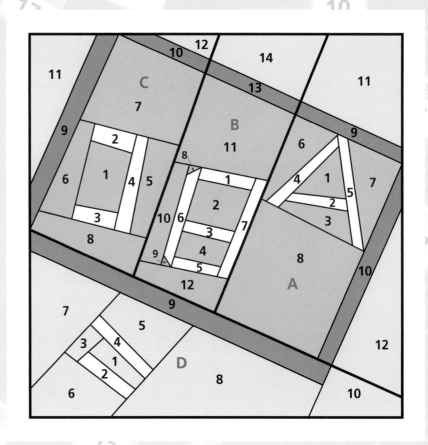

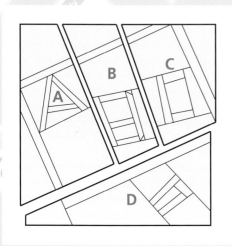

Jack-o-Lantern

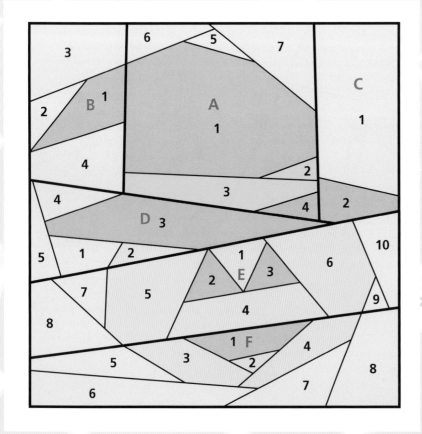

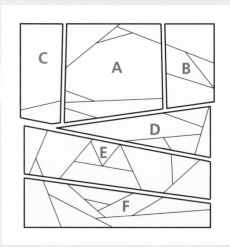

Leaf & Acorn

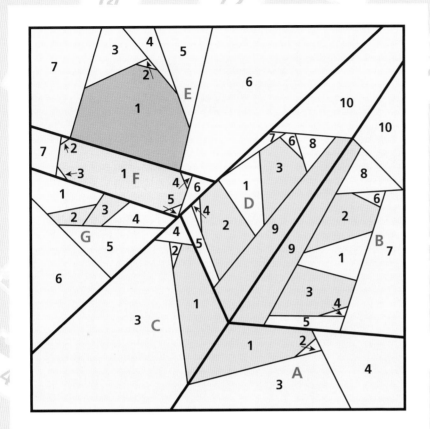

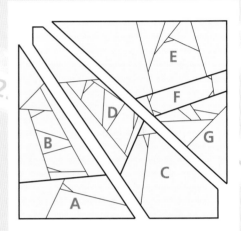

Angel

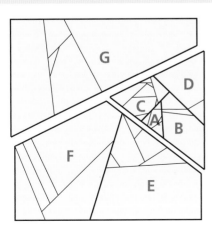

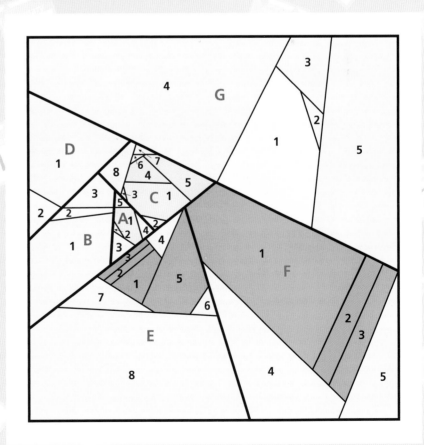

Star Blocks

Pinwheel Star Bed Quilt

Use our Materials and Cutting lists to make a bed quilt, a wall hanging or a miniature quilt from the "Pinwheel Star" pattern, or choose any of the other 11 star blocks to make your project.

Pinwheel Star Bed Quilt

Size: 66" x 80"
Number of Blocks: 20

Block: Pinwheel Star (page 41)
Block Size: 14" finished

MATERIALS

1 yard each, light purple, yellow, dark green, cream 1, cream 2
$1^3/4$ yards dark purple
1 yard blue (includes first border)
1 yard medium green (includes second border)
1 yard reddish purple (includes third border)
$5^1/2$ yards backing
$5/8$ yard green (binding)

CUTTING

8 strips, $1^1/2$"-wide, blue (first border)
8 strips, 2"-wide, medium green (second border)
8 strips, 3"-wide strips, reddish purple (third border)
8 strips, $2^1/2$"-wide strips, dark green (binding)

Pinwheel Star Wall Hanging

Size: 30" x 30"
Number of Blocks: 16

Block: Pinwheel Star (page 41)
Block Size: 6" finished

MATERIALS

Fat quarters of assorted purple, red, yellow, cream, beige batiks
$1/4$ yard dark purple batik (first border)
$5/8$ yard light purple batik (second border, binding)
1 yard backing

CUTTING

2 strips, $1^1/2$" x $24^1/2$", dark purple (first border)
2 strips, $1^1/2$" x $26^1/2$", dark purple (first border)
2 strips, $2^1/2$" x $26^1/2$", light purple (second border)
2 strips, $2^1/2$" x $30^1/2$", light purple (second border)
4 strips, $2^1/2$"-wide, light purple (binding)

Pinwheel Star Miniature

Size: $13^1/2$" x $16^1/2$"
Number of Blocks: 12

Block: Pinwheel Star (page 41)
Block Size: 3" finished

MATERIALS

Fat quarters of pink (includes second border), yellow, and green
$1/2$ yard white print (includes first border)
$1/4$ yard blue (includes third border, binding)

CUTTING

2 strips, 1" x $12^1/2$", white print (first border)
2 strips, 1" x $10^1/2$", white print (first border)
2 strips, $1^1/4$" x $13^1/2$", pink (second border)
2 strips, $1^1/4$" x 12", pink (second border)
2 strips, $1^1/2$" x 15", blue (third border)
2 strips, $1^1/2$" x 14", blue (third border)
2 strips, $2^1/2$"-wide, blue (binding)

Pinwheel Star Wall Hanging

Pinwheel Star Miniature

Shaded Star

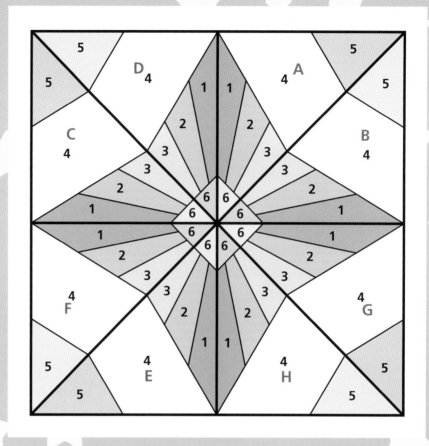

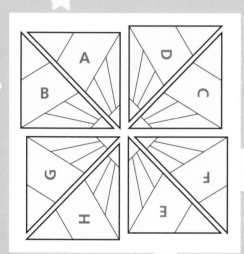

4-Pointed Star

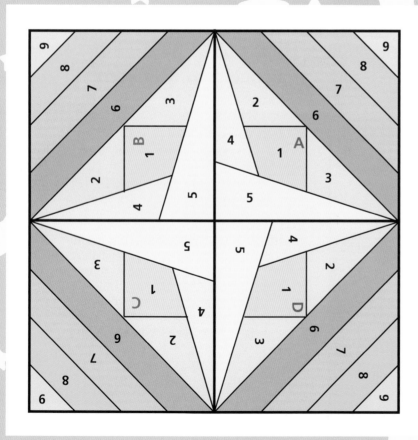

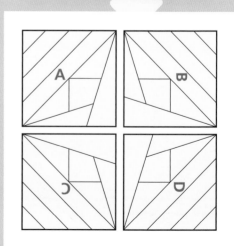

Pinwheel Star

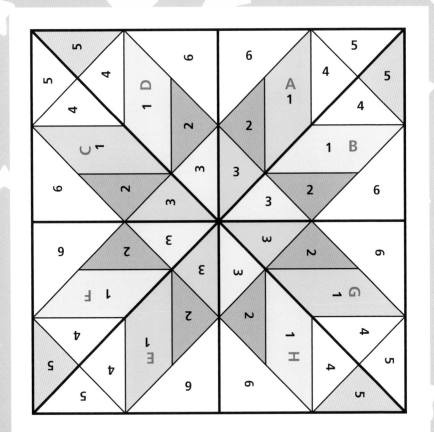

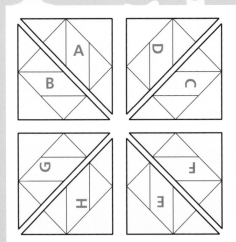

Whirligig Star

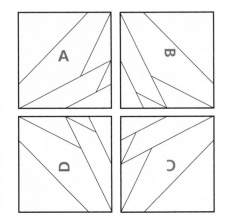

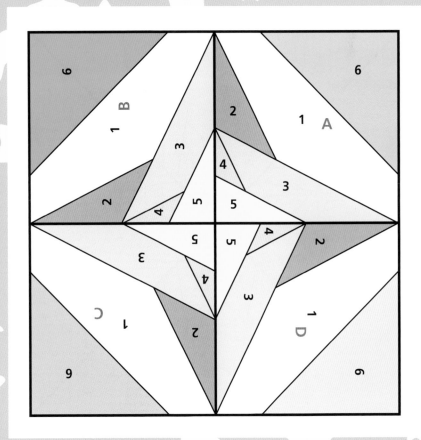

Star Jewel

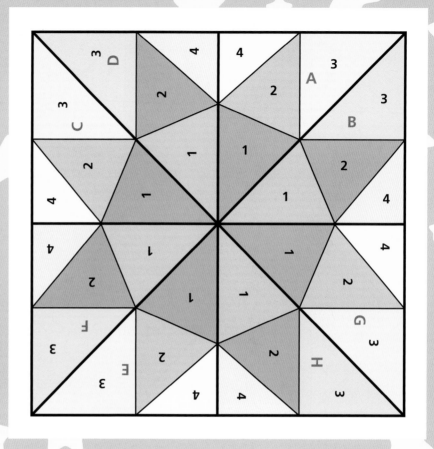

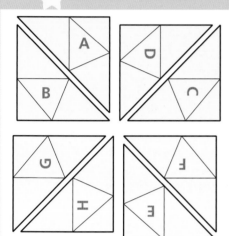

Star Cross

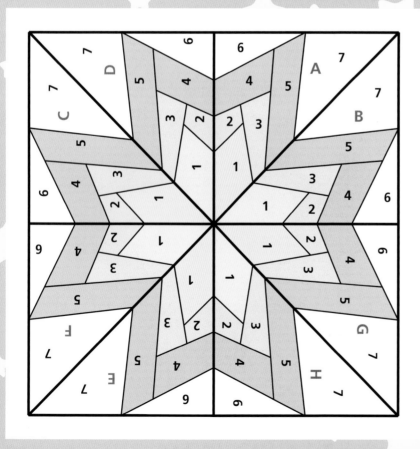

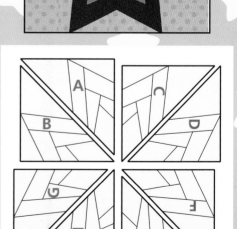

Patriotic Star

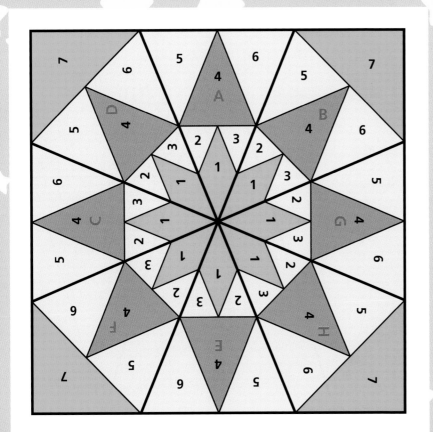

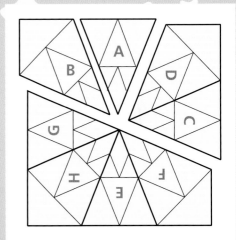

Pointy Star

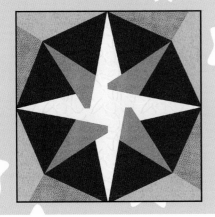

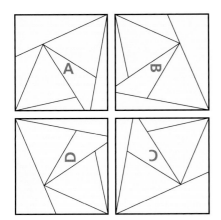

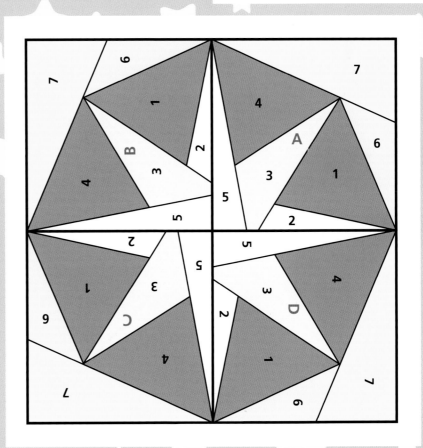

5-Pointed Star

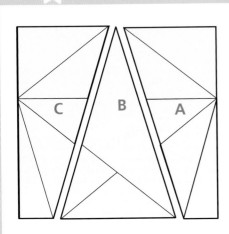

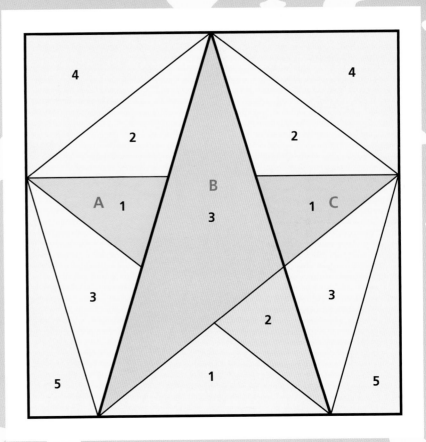

American Star

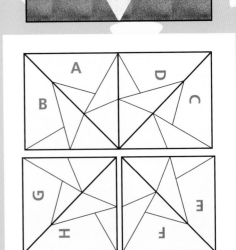

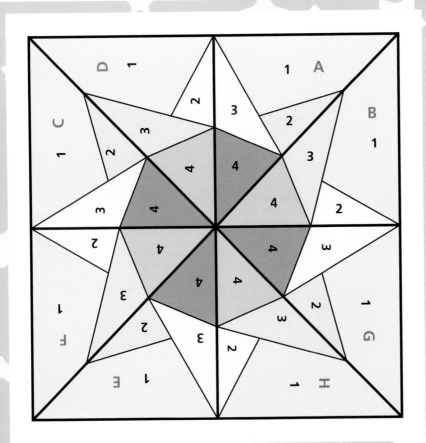

Kaleidoscope Star

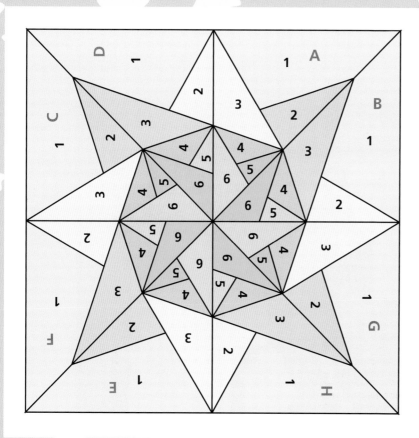

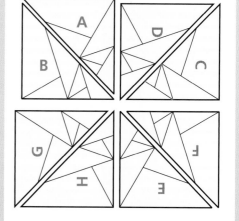

Uneven Star

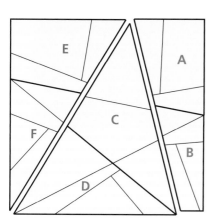

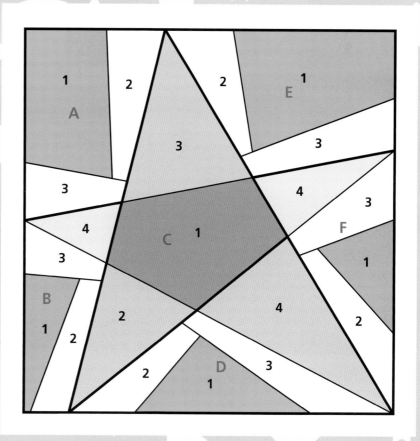

Christmas Blocks

Christmas Wall Hanging

Christmas Wall Hanging

Approximate Size: 45″ x 45″

Blocks: (pages 48 to 53)
- 1 Angel (6" finished)
- 3 Christmas Lights (4" finished)
- 1 Santa (6" finished)
- 1 Candy Cane (6" finished)
- 1 Candle (6" finished)
- 1 Stocking (6" finished)
- 1 Ornaments (8" finished)
- 1 Sleigh (8" finished)
- 1 Presents (8" finished)
- 2 "Noel" (6" finished)
- 1 Wreath (6" finished)
- 1 Tree (6" finished)

MATERIALS

Fat quarters of red, white
Scraps of yellow, orange, blue, peach, light green, dark green, white/silver
$6^{1}/2$" x $6^{1}/2$" square brown (tree trunk)
1 yard green print 1 (block background)
$3/4$ yard blue print 1 (block background)
$3/8$ yard red print (first border, cornerstones)
$5/8$ yard blue print 2 (plain blocks)
$3/4$ yard green print 2 (second border, binding)
$2^{1}/4$ yards backing

CUTTING

2 rectangles, $6^{1}/2$" x $4^{1}/2$", blue print 2
2 rectangles, $3^{1}/2$" x $6^{1}/2$", blue print 2
6 rectangles, $9^{1}/2$" x $6^{1}/2$", blue print 2
2 strips, $6^{1}/2$" x $24^{1}/2$", blue print 2
4 strips, 2"-wide, red print (first border)
4 squares, $3^{1}/2$" x $3^{1}/2$", red print (cornerstones)
4 strips, $3^{1}/2$"-wide, green print 2 (second border)
5 strips, $2^{1}/2$"-wide, green print 2 (binding)

Celebrate the season by using any or all of these Christmas patterns to add a bit of creativity to your holiday decorating.

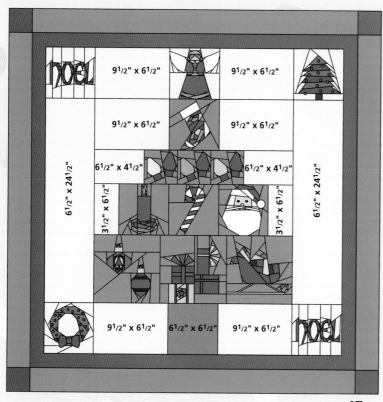

Christmas Wall Hanging Layout

Christmas Tree

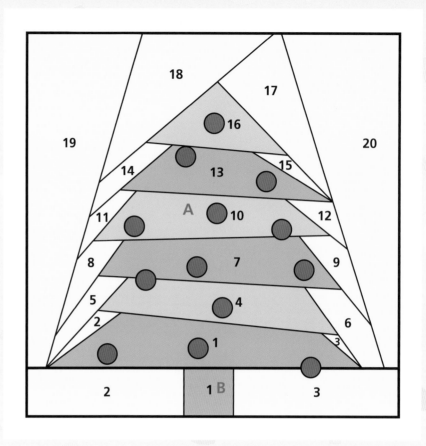

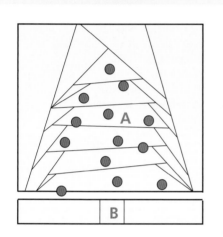

Christmas Candle

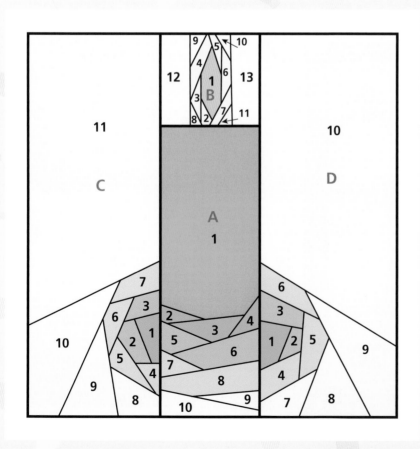

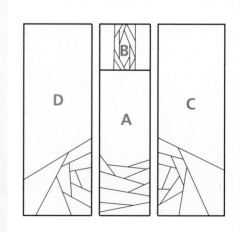

Candy Cane

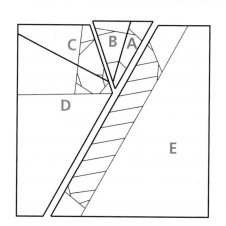

(Candy Cane pattern — top-left diagram labels:)
13 11 4 4 5 6
3 B 4 C
A 3
10 1 1 6
12 2 1
8 2 2 3 6
6 2 1
4 3
D
2 5
1
7
E 3
17 5
7
9 14
15 16

Christmas Angel

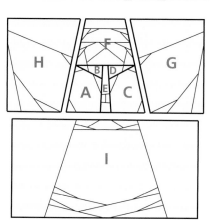

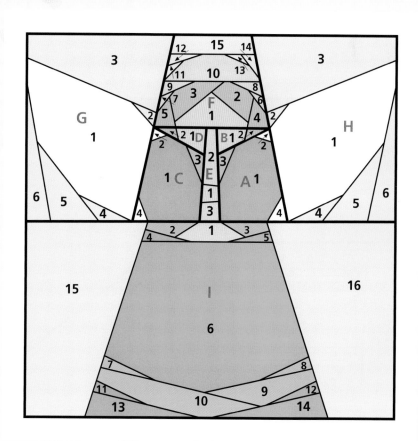

49

Christmas Gifts

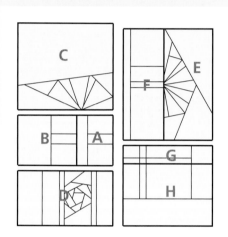

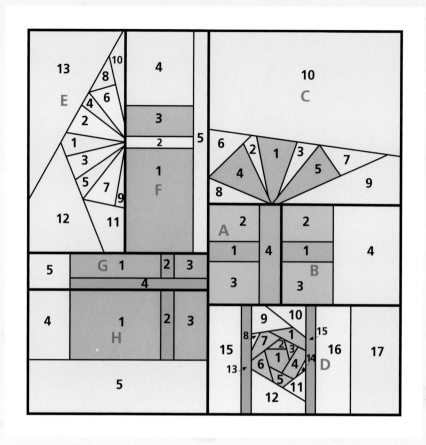

Ornaments

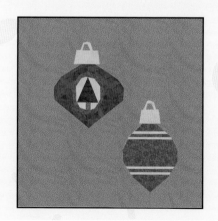

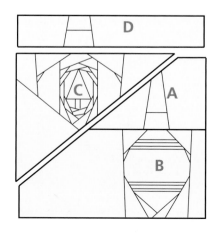

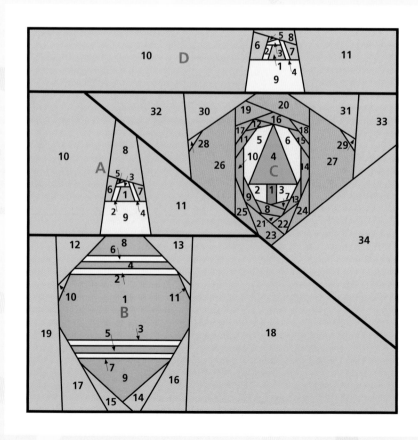

Noel

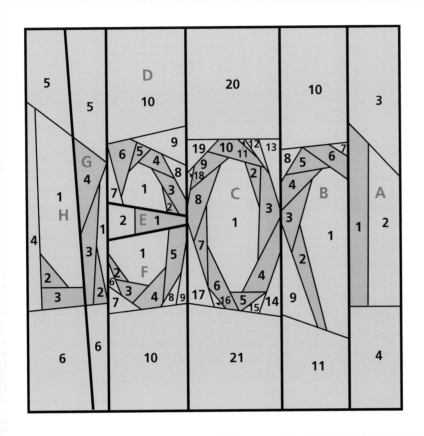

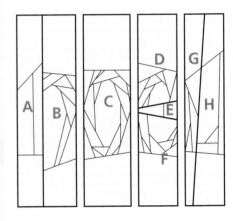

Wreath

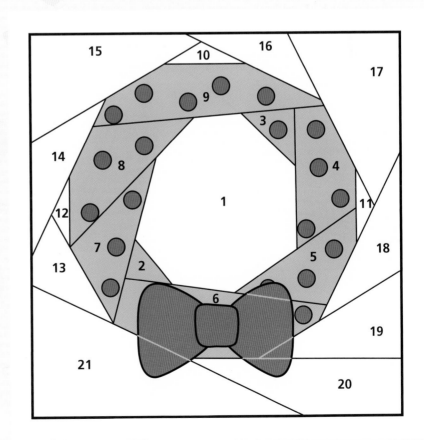

Santa's Sleigh

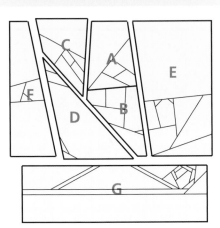

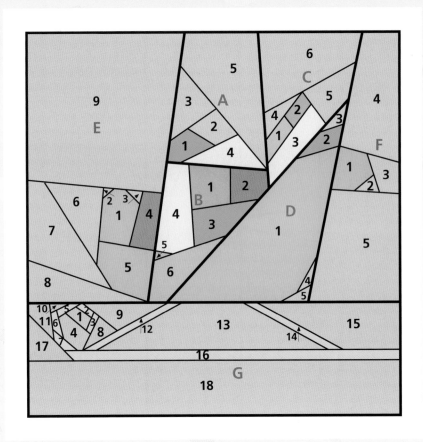

Santa

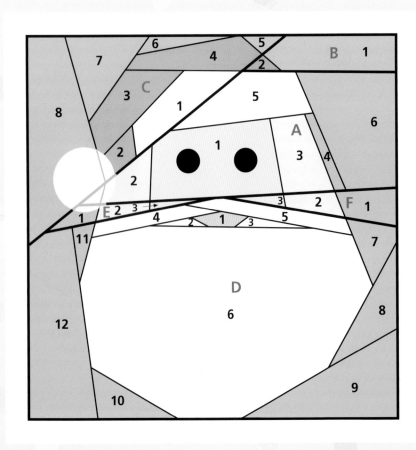

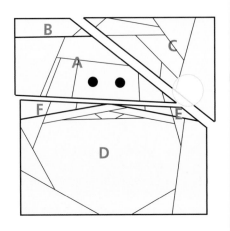

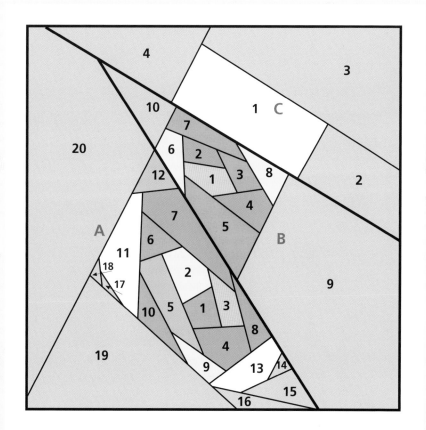

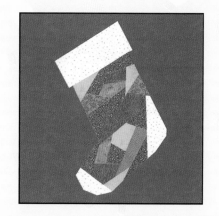

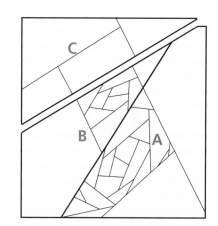

Christmas Lights

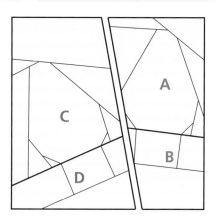

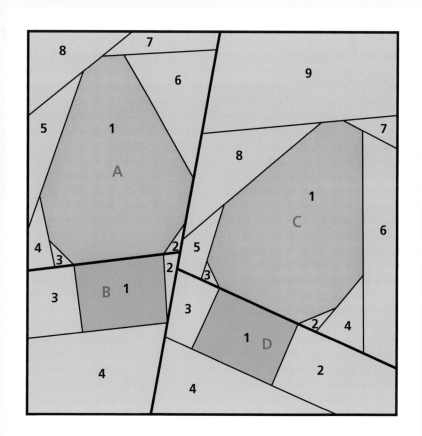

Garden Blocks

Whether it's tulips or pansies, potted posies or potted buds; a humming-bird or a bumble bee, you'll find patterns for them here.

Tulip

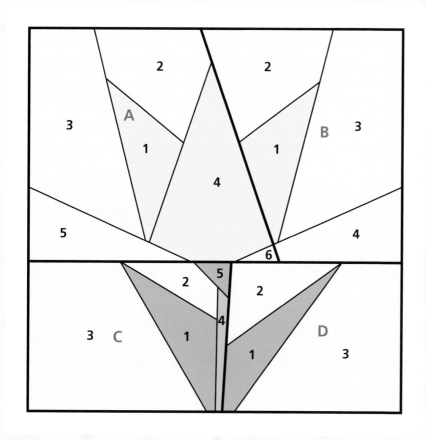

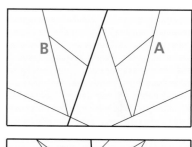

Garden Tools

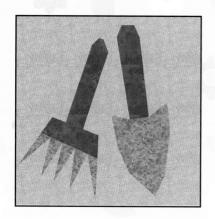

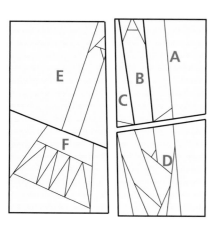

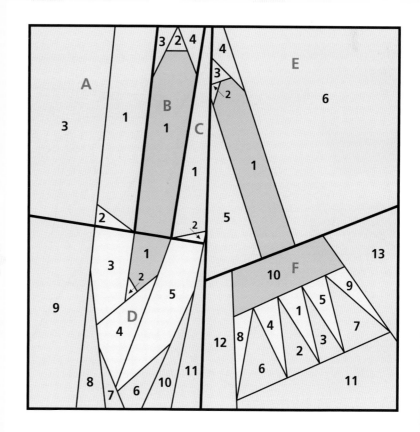

55

Potted Posies

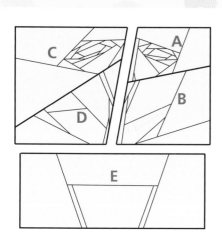

E

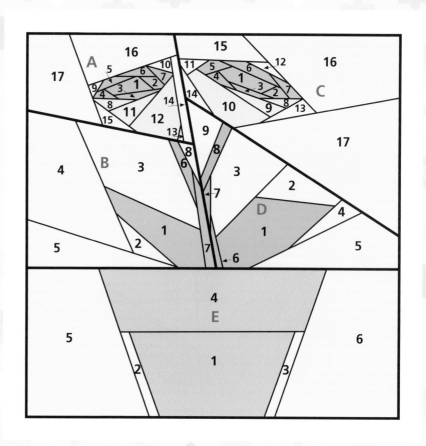

Watering Can

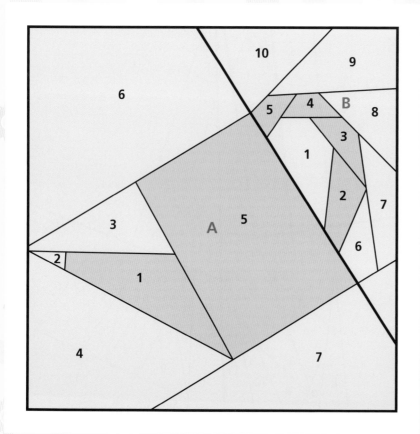

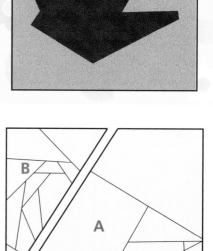

Flying Butterfly

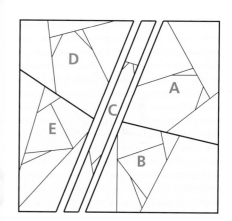

Butterfly

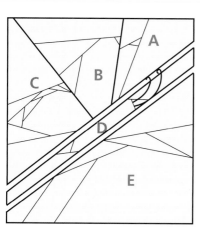

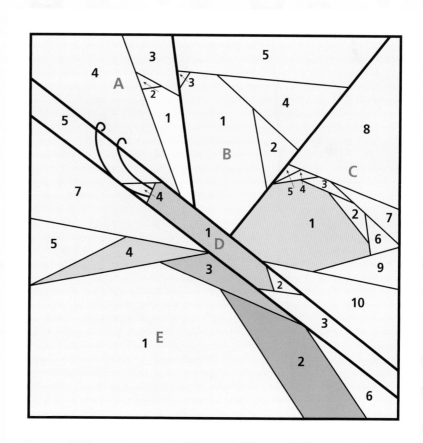

Tulip Bouquet

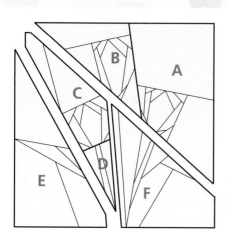

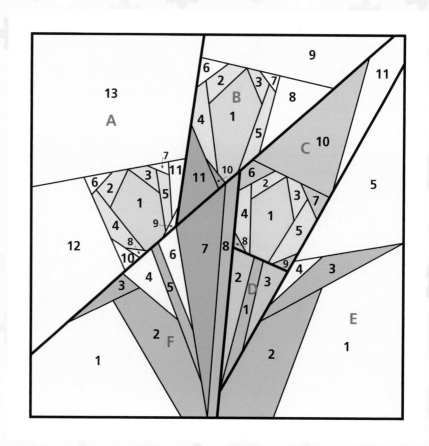

Snail

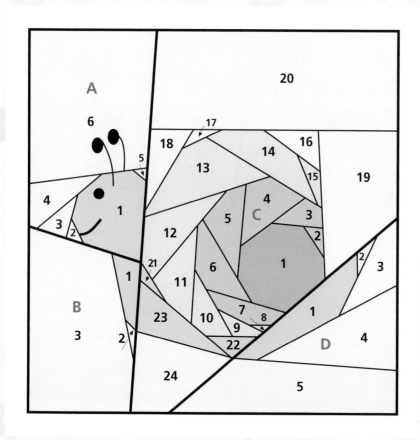

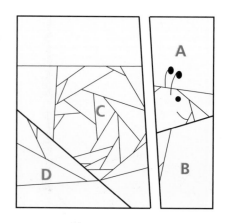

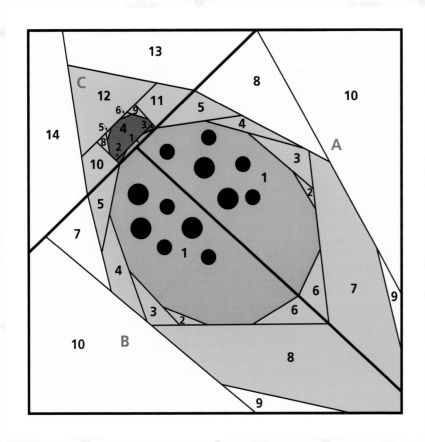

13

C

12   11

14   6 9
      5 3
      4 1   5
      8 2
             4   4

10

5   3

7   2   1

4

3   6

2   6   7   8   9

10   B

8

9

Ladybug

Ladybug

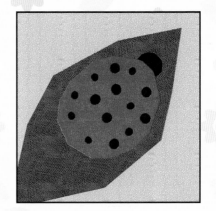

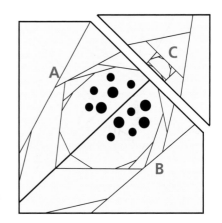

A

C

B

Frog

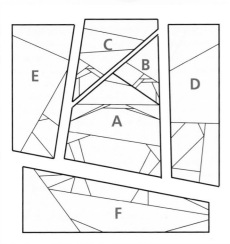

E

C

B

A   D

F

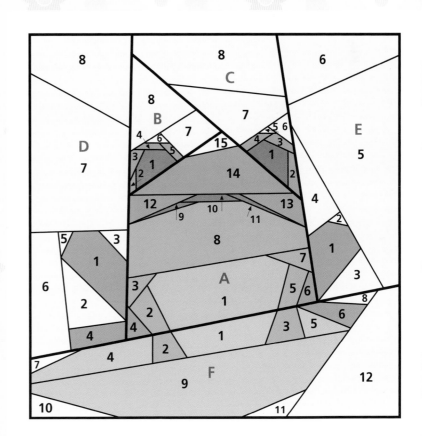

8   8   6

              C

      8   7
      B
         7
   4 6   4 5 6
   3   5   15   4 3
   1   1
D 1 2   2
7   14
                      13   4
   12   9 10 11
5   3   8   1
1   7   2
6   1 3
   2   3   5 6
      2   6
      4 4   1
         2   3 5   8
7   4   1   6
   10   F   11   12
      9

Bee Hive

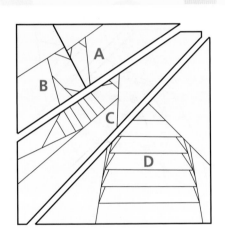

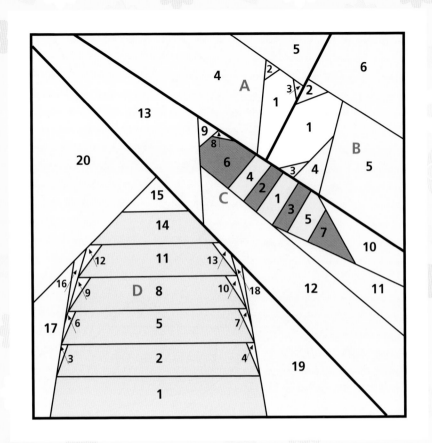

Bumble Bee

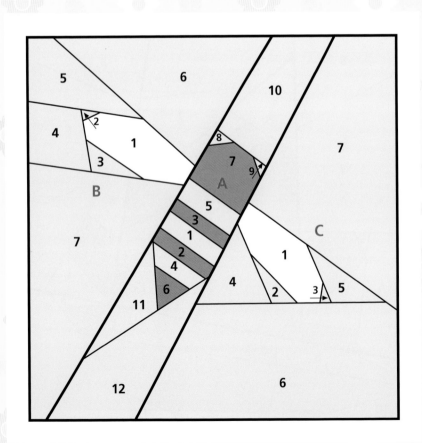

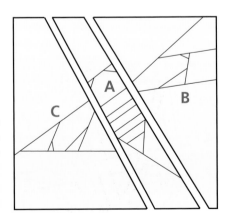

Pansies

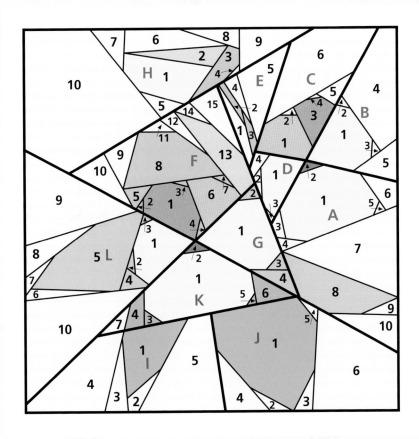

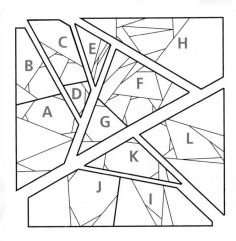

Red Posy

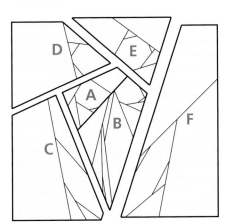

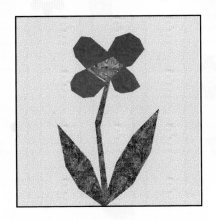

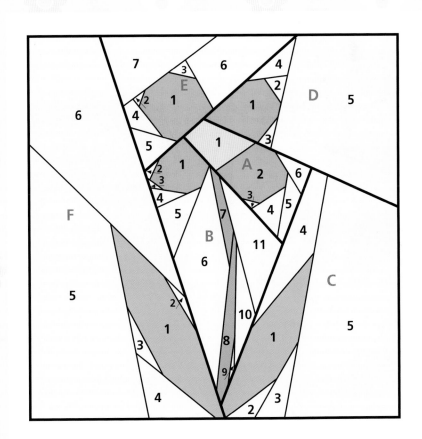

Potted Buds

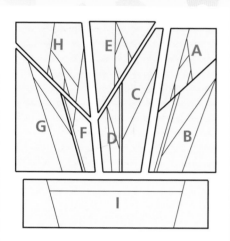

Seed Packets

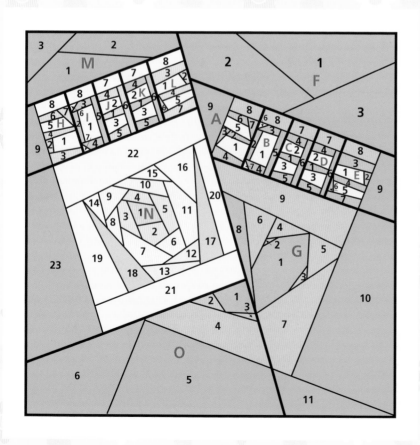

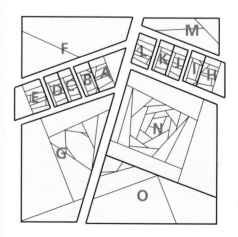

Hummingbird

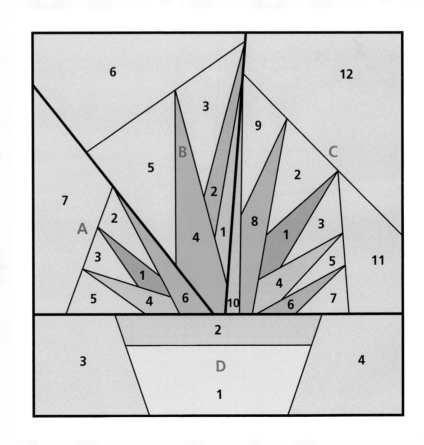

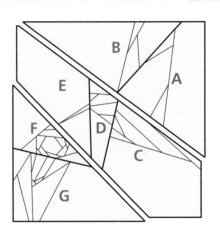

Potted Plant

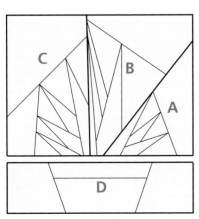

Flower

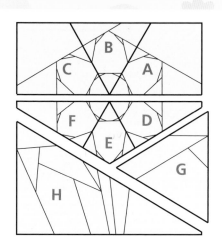

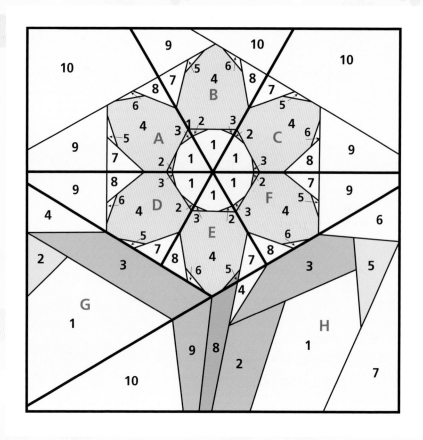

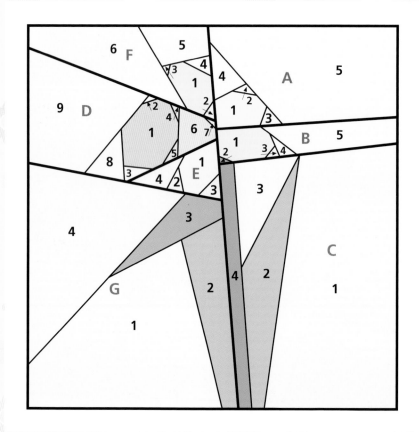

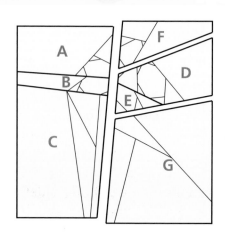

64

Foundation Piecing

Materials

Before you begin, decide the kind of foundation on which you are planning to piece the blocks.

Since the blocks in this book are printed from a CD using your computer and printer, the most popular choice for a foundation is regular copy paper since it is readily available. You can also use freezer paper. It comes in sheets by C. Jenkins or a roll by Reynolds®. If you use the roll, you will have to cut sheets that will fit through your printer. If using freezer paper, be sure to print the pattern on the dull side. Then as you piece, use a small craft iron or a travel iron to press fabric pieces in place on the foundation after sewing each seam. The paper is removed once the blocks are completely sewn.

There are other options for foundation materials that can be used with your computer and printer. One type is Tear Away™ or Fun-da-tion™, translucent non-woven materials, combining the advantages of both paper and fabric. They are easy to see through, and like paper, they can be removed with ease. Another foundation material is one that dissolves in water after use called Dissolve Away Foundation Paper by EZ Quilting®.

Preparing the Foundation

Since the Block Patterns are given in several sizes on a CD, preparing your foundation is easier than ever. All you need to do is decide which block you would like to make (from 2" to 8" square) and which size you will need for your quilt. Place the CD in your computer, choose the block and print the number of copies that you will need for your quilt.

The blocks on the CD range in size from 2" to 8" square since those are the sizes that will fit on a regular sheet of paper. For those that are larger than an 8½" x 11" sheet of paper, you may need to go to your local copier store to print the blocks on 11" x 15" paper. See Frequently Asked Questions on the CD for guidelines on printing blocks over 8" square.

Cutting the Fabric

In foundation piecing, you do not have to cut perfect shapes! You can, therefore, use odd pieces of fabric: squares, strips, and rectangles. The one thing you must remember, however, is that every piece must be at least ¼" larger on all sides than the space it is going to cover. Strips and squares are easy: just measure the length and width of the needed space and add ½" all around. Cut your strip to that measurement. Triangles, however, can be a bit tricky. In that case, measure the widest point of the triangle and cut your fabric about ½" to 1" wider.

Other Supplies for Foundation Piecing

You will need a cleaned and oiled sewing machine, glue stick, pins, paper scissors, fabric scissors, and foundation material.

Before beginning to sew your actual block by machine, determine the proper stitch length. Use a piece of the paper you are planning to use for the foundation and draw a straight line on it. Set your machine so that it sews with a fairly short stitch (about 20 stitches per inch). Sew along the line. If you can tear the paper apart with ease, you are sewing with the right length. You don't want to sew with such a short stitch that the paper falls apart by itself.

Using a Pattern

The numbers on the block show the order in which the pieces are to be placed and sewn on the foundation. It is extremely important that you follow the numbers; otherwise the entire process won't work.

Making the Block

The important thing to remember about making a foundation block is that the fabric goes on the unmarked side of the foundation while you sew on the printed side. The finished block is a mirror image of the original pattern.

Step 1: Hold the foundation up to a light source—even a window—with the unmarked side facing. Find the space marked 1 on the unmarked side and put a dab of glue there. Place the fabric right side up on the unmarked side on Space 1, making certain that the fabric overlaps at least ¼" on all sides of space 1. **(Diagram 1)**

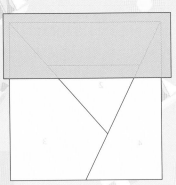

Diagram 1

Step 2: Fold the foundation along the line between Space 1 and Space 2. Cut the fabric so that it is ¼" from the fold. **(Diagram 2)**

Diagram 2

Step 3: With right sides together, place Fabric Piece 2 on Fabric Piece 1, making sure that the edge of Piece 2 is even with the just-trimmed edge of Piece 1. **(Diagram 3)**

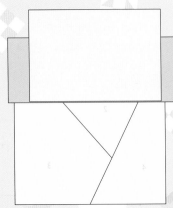

Diagram 3

Step 4: To make certain that Piece 2 will cover Space 2, fold the fabric piece back along the line between Space 1 and Space 2. **(Diagram 4)**

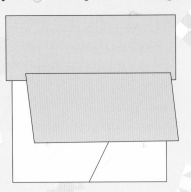

Diagram 4

Step 5: With the marked side of the foundation facing up, place the piece on the sewing machine (or sew by hand), holding both Piece 1 and Piece 2 in place. Sew along the line between Space 1 and Space 2. **(Diagram 5)**

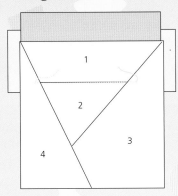

Diagram 5

Hint: *If you use a small stitch, it will be easier to remove the paper later. Start stitching about two or three stitches before the beginning of the line and end your sewing two or three stitches beyond the line, allowing the stitches to be held in place by the next round of stitching rather than by backstitching.*

Step 6: Turn the work over and open Piece 2. Press the seam open. **(Diagram 6)**

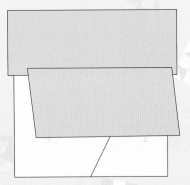

Diagram 6

Step 7: Turning the work so that the marked side is on top, fold the foundation forward along the line between Space 1+2 and Space 3. Trim about ⅛" to ¼" from the fold. It is easier to trim the paper if you pull the paper away from the stitching. If you use fabric as your foundation, fold the fabric forward as far as it will go and then start to trim. **(Diagram 7)**

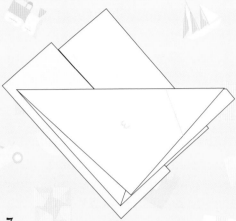

Diagram 7

Step 8: Place Fabric #3 right side down even with the just-trimmed edge. **(Diagram 8)**

Diagram 8

Step 9: Turn the block over to the marked side and sew along the line between Space 1+2 and Space 3. **(Diagram 9)**

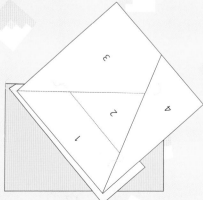

Diagram 9

Step 10: Turn the work over, open Piece 3 and press the seam. **(Diagram 10)**

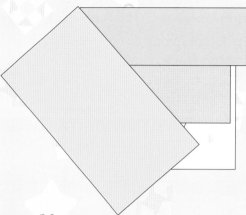

Diagram 10

Step 11: In the same way you have added the other pieces, add Piece #4 to complete this block. Trim the fabric ¼" from the edge of the foundation. The foundation-pieced block is completed. **(Diagram 11)**

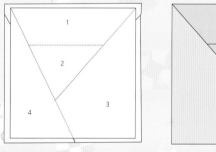
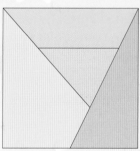

Diagram 11

After you have finished sewing a block, don't immediately remove the paper. Since you are often piecing with tiny bits of fabric, grainline is not a factor. Therefore, some of the pieces may have been cut on the bias and may have a tendency to stretch. You can eliminate any problem with distortion by keeping the paper in place until all of the blocks have been sewn together. If, however, you want to remove the paper, stay stitch along the outer edge of the block to help keep the block in shape.

Sewing Multiple Sections

Many of the blocks in foundation piecing are created with two or more sections. These sections, which are indicated by letters, are individually pieced and then sewn together. The cutting line for these sections is indicated by a bold line. Before you start to make any of these multi-

67

section blocks, begin by cutting the foundation piece apart so that each section is worked independently. Leave a ¼" seam allowance around each section.

Step 1: Following the previous instructions for Making the Block, complete each section. Then place the sections right side together. Pin the corners of the top section to the corners of the bottom section. **(Diagram 12)**

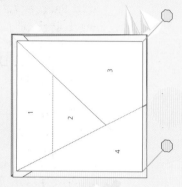

Diagram 12

Step 2: If you are certain that the pieces are aligned correctly, sew the two sections together using the regular stitch length on the sewing machine.

Step 3: Press the sections open and continue sewing the sections in pairs. **(Diagram 13)**

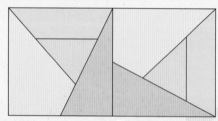

Diagram 13

Step 4: Sew necessary pairs of sections together to complete the block. **(Diagram 14)**

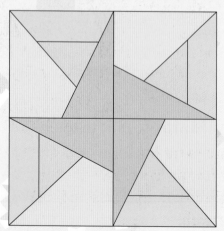

Diagram 14

What You Don't Want to Forget

1. If you plan to sew by hand, begin by taking some backstitches that will anchor the thread at the beginning of the line. Then use a backstitch every four of five stitches. End the stitching with a few backstitches.

2. If you plan to sew by machine, start stitching two or three stitches before the start of the stitching line and finish your stitching two or three stitches beyond the end.

3. Use a short stitch (about 20 stitches per inch) for paper foundations to make it easier to remove the paper. If the paper falls apart as you sew, your stitches are too short.

4. Press each seam as you finish it.

5. Stitching which goes from a space into another space will not interfere with adding additional fabric pieces.

6. Remember to trim all seam allowances at least ¼".

7. When sewing points, start from the wide end and sew towards the point.

8. Unless you plan to use it only once in the block, it is a good idea to stay away from directional prints in foundation piecing.

9. When cutting pieces for foundation piecing, never worry about the grainline.

10. Always remember to sew on the marked side, placing the fabric on the unmarked side.

11. Follow the numerical order, or it won't work.

12. Once you have finished making a block do not remove the paper until the entire quilt has been finished unless you stay stitch around the outside of the block.

13. Be sure that the ink you use to make your foundation is permanent and will not wash out into your fabric.